Border Knight

Carol Dixon

'This 8th Henry, son to the 7th Henry, bounteous and good,
His father yet living, was a right valiant knight,
and did many noticeable acts as becomes his noble bloud,
For defence of his prince's realm he spared not to fight;
for his sharp quickness and speedinesse in need
Henry Hottespur he was called indeed.
In York Minster this most honourable knight
By the first Earl, his father, lyeth openly in sight.'

Contents

Foreword..2
Part 1 - 1366-1378 - Early Years...3
Part II - 1382-1387 - Military Training..9
Part III - 1388 - The Battle of Otterburn..13
Part IV - 1390-1399 - Expeditions Abroad...19
Part V - 1399 - Bolingbroke's Rebellion...23
Part VI - 1400-1402 - Scotland and Wales..27
Part VII - 1402 - The Battle of Homildon 31
Part VIII - 1403 - The Battle of Shrewsbury..35
Properties Held by the Percies..44
The Percies as Border Wardens..45
Genealogy..46
Bibliography..47
Places to visit..48

Foreword

In writing this biography of the life of Harry Hotspur I must stress that I am not a historian, rather an interested local. I was born in Hotspur Place, Alnwick and for the first few years of my life passed Hotspur Tower daily. I was educated at the old Duchess's Grammar School (opposite the Castle) and for six years wore the badge of the Percies on my blazer and the Percy crest on my beret.

Most of the information I have collated is from local sources and I should like to acknowledge the assistance of the Northumberland County Library Service, Mr Colin Shrimpton, Librarian at Alnwick Castle, Prof. Andrew Hamnett for the translation of part of King James of Cyprus' letter to King Richard II, and my husband for taking the photographs.

Carol Dixon

2nd edition 2016

Hotspur Tower

Part 1 - 1366-1378 - Early Years

In the north of England the name 'Harry Hotspur' evokes a kind of local pride similar to that of Robin Hood around Nottingham or Hereward the Wake in the Fen country. Hotspur was immortalised by William Shakespeare in his historical plays, Richard II and Henry IV Part 1. Born into the illustrious House of Percy, Dukes of Northumberland, he fought in the infamous battle of Otterburn, was the victor of the Battle of Homildon, and died on the battlefield at Shrewsbury, in rebellion against his half-cousin, Henry Bolingbroke, King Henry IV.

Harry Hotspur was born, Henry Percy, on the 20th of May 1366[1] at Alnwick Castle in Northumberland. He was the eldest son and heir of Henry, 4th Lord Percy who acceded to the dukedom in 1368 on the death of his father, Henry, 3rd Lord Percy - distinguished knight of the battles of Crecy, Poitiers, and Neville's Cross.

Harry's mother was Margaret Neville, daughter of Ralph Neville, 4th Lord Raby of Raby Castle in County Durham. Through his paternal grandmother, Lady Mary Plantagenet, granddaughter of King Henry III, his family was closely linked with the Royal Family. King Henry II had 2 sons - Edward, later King Edward I (nicknamed Longshanks) who, after his incursions into Scotland, was known as the Hammer of the Scots and a younger son, Edmund (nicknamed Crouchback), the father of Henry, Duke of Lancaster and Mary Plantagenet.[2]

Harry's father, Henry was brought up in the household of his uncle, the Duke of Lancaster, as was the custom at the time, and was educated at court with the royal princes, his half-cousins. Henry Percy became particularly friendly with the prince nearest in age to himself - John of Gaunt, who was third in line to the throne after his elder brothers, Edward, the Black Prince, and Lionel, Duke of Clarence. Even closer links were forged between the two when John married Henry's cousin Blanche, the daughter of Henry of Lancaster and, on her father's death, John assumed the title Duke of Lancaster by right of his marriage, and inherited all the lands belonging to the House of Lancaster. It was their eldest son, Henry Bolingbroke (born 1366 or 1367) who in 1399 usurped the throne from his cousin, Richard II, son of the Black Prince.

---

[1] His own evidence at the Scrope/Grosvenor trial

[2] See Genealogy section - page 46

Childhood

Little is known about Harry Hotspur's childhood. It is assumed that he was brought up in his early years at Warkworth castle, a favourite seat of the Percies at the time, and at Alnwick, their northern stronghold where his father, the Duke (and in his absence, the Duchess) would hold court to listen to the grievances of local tenants, bring lawbreakers to trial etc.

It is quite likely that the whole household travelled around their other estates from time to time, particularly those in Yorkshire - Leconfield, near Beverley, Topcliffe in the vale of York, and Spofforth and Poklington, in Wharfedale. It was usual for the gentry to move from manor to manor three or four times a year, in order to oversee the smooth running of the family estates. It is possible that Harry may even have been taken to Petworth Manor in Sussex or to their house in London but it is more likely he was older before he made the longer journeys. Travelling at that time was very slow and involved as the whole household moved, not only with their large retinue of men at arms, servants, personal maids etc but also all of their baggage and most of their furniture.

Harry had 3 brothers and one sister: Thomas who died in 1386 (married Elizabeth, daughter of David Strathbogie, Earl of Atoll); Ralph who lost his life in the Holy Land in 1399 (married Philippa Strathbogie, sister of Elizabeth); Margaret (who may have married Sir Ralph Fenwick); and Alan, about whom there is no information recorded so it is assumed he died in infancy.

Alnwick Abbey Gatehouse

Like most of their contemporaries, the Percies were devout in their faith, attending mass regularly in the chapels of their castles and receiving the Host (Communion) before going into battle. Shortly after his wife's death, Harry's father made a bequest to the Premonstratension monks of Alnwick abbey in her memory for masses to be said for her soul, and for the safe keeping of himself and his children. Shortly afterwards Harry and his brothers, Ralph and Thomas, were admitted to the fraternity of the abbey as lay brothers which entitled them to live in the abbey at the end of their lives and be buried in a monk's habit in the abbey cemetery if they so wished – this, as was the belief in those days, would assure their souls a place in heaven.

In the year 1376 Lord Percy purchased from King Edward III a licence to annexe St Leonard's hospice to the abbey and later in the year he granted the Carmelite friars of Hulne Priory free fishing rights in the river Aln. Harry, from his own purse, donated gifts of white samite robes for the celebrant and a set of altar adornments.

In 1372 Harry's mother died and he became a page in his father's service, accompanying him to France during the campaigns of 1373/4, led by King Edward III and his sons. The Percies - Henry and his brother Thomas, who was Admiral of England at the time - served under John of Gaunt. Unlike the great English victories of Crecy (1346) and Poitiers (1356) in the early part of the Hundred Years' War with France, these campaigns against the du Guesculin brothers met with limited success and it was not long before Harry and his father returned to their normal haunts on the Borders. Their involvement however helped to further their political careers, Sir Thomas Percy, for instance, later became Ambassador to France and Spain, and it proved to be a good training ground for Harry to learn the craft of warfare.

In April 1377 Harry was knighted, along with John of Gaunt's son, Henry Bolingbroke, by Richard, the only surviving son of the Black Prince who had died the previous year. Richard, the heir to the throne, had just received his knighthood from his grandfather, the aged and ailing King Edward III. At the same time Harry's father was created Earl of Northumberland and admitted to the Order of the Garter as was his brother Sir Thomas Percy, who became Earl of Worcester. One of the Earl of Northumberland's first duties, a few month's later as Earl Marshall of England, was to preside at the ten-year-old King Richard's coronation which took place in London on July 16th 1377 and Harry was present at the occasion in Westminster Abbey.

First Battle

On the 30th November 1378 a raiding party of Scots managed to capture the castle of Berwick upon Tweed on the border of England and Scotland. They killed the Constable, Sir Robert de Boynton, and only allowed his family to go

Berwick Castle

free on the promise of a ransom of 2000 marks. At the time Earl Percy, who was Governor of Berwick, was meeting with the Scottish knight, Sir John Gordon, in Berwick town to discuss and armistice to try and bring an end to the incessant border raiding which was crippling the town and countryside around on both sides of the border. Seemingly about 40 raiders, spearheaded by a group of 8 ringleaders (said to be under the command of Sir Alexander Ramsay of Lothian) had somehow effected an entry by one of the towers and this incursion put an abrupt end to the peace negotiations.

'Hot Spur'

Earl Percy immediately ordered the castle to be besieged and led an assault himself against the main gate, assisted by stone-throwing catapults. He divided the remainder of his forces into three under Sir Alan de Heton, Sir Thomas de Ilderton, and members of the Heron family, to assail the other three gates while he and Harry kept up the attack on the main gate. After a siege of 8 days, during which time engineers had tunnelled under the gates, all parties attacked the castle simultaneously and, after a struggle lasting more than two hours, 12 year old Harry, at the head of his father's troops, managed to gain entry to the castle. Such was the ferocity of his attack that tradition has it he was nicknamed 'Hot Spur' and so the young Sir Harry 'Hotspur' first distinguished himself by the personal courage for which he was later to become famous.

Percy Banner

Warkworth Castle - Medieval Home of the Percy Family

Warkworth Castle Keep from the Gatehouse

Stairs to the Great Hall

Anteroom (visitors' waiting area) with view of river Coquet

The Great Hall

Chapel

The solar (private chamber) with view of St Lawrence's Church

Warkworth Castle is now in the care of English Heritage

Part II - 1382-1387 - Military Training

At the end of 1381 Roger Mortimer, Earl of March, died. His wife Phillippa (who died in 1378) was the daughter of Lionel, Duke of Clarence (the Black Prince's brother) and their children, Elizabeth, Roger and Edmund, as grandchildren of king Edward III, became royal wards.

In 1383 the wardship of the Mortimer lands was acquired by the Earls of Arundel, Warwick, and Northumberland and the Mortimer children were betrothed to members of their families. Nine-year-old Roger, became heir to the throne, and was married later in the year to Eleanor Holland, daughter of the king's uncle Thomas, Earl of Kent, who had purchased Roger's wardship from the Earl of Arundel. Elizabeth, aged about eleven or twelve, was betrothed to Harry Hotspur and her portion of lands in North Wales passed into the Percy family to be held as her dowry.

It is assumed that she moved to Alnwick Castle at this time, as her future sisters-in-law, Elizabeth and Phillippa Strathbogie – the daughters and heiresses of the Earl of Atholl, did upon their engagements to Harry's brothers, Thomas and Ralph Percy.

Military Training

In 1383 Harry, serving with his uncle, Sir Thomas Percy, ambassador to France and Spain, accompanied the Bishop of Norwich, Hugh Despenser on a military expedition to Flanders. This abortive campaign, classed as a crusade or Holy War, took place upon the instigation of Pope Urban VI to try and oust the 'anti-pope' Clement whom the French supported during the period known as the Great Schism in the Church when, for many years, there were two popes - one in Rome and the other in Avignon.

In 1384 Harry assisted his father for a time as Warden of the East and West Marches towards Scotland where they worked as guardians of the Borders, keeping law and order and sitting in judgement, along with their Scottish counterparts, on Marcher days. On 20th May 1385 he was commissioned as Warden of the East March in place of his father and was created Governor of Berwick by the king. In August King Richard himself led an unsuccessful incursion into Scotland and Harry accompanied him (commanding 100 men-at-arms and 100 archers) serving in the rearguard of which the Earl of Northumberland was commander-in-chief.

Exploits in France

In 1386, when the Earl of Northumberland was Admiral of the Northern Fleet and was expected to keep the North Sea free from Scots and French pirates, Harry and his brother Ralph were sent to Great Yarmouth with some of their border troops since an attack was expected on Calais which was in English hands. Rumours were rife at the time about a supposed French invasion of the English coast but it never materialized. After weeks of inactivity Harry commandeered a fleet of fishing vessels and sailed to France where the Northumbrians made lightning raids on the French countryside to such an extent that the French also took up his name of 'Hotesporre'. A contemporary writer described him as "this Henry is by the French and Scots called Harre Hotesporre because in the silence of the starry night, others being unoccupied and in quiet sleep, he laboured unwearied as if his spur was hot"!

French Ships

In August, Harry, in command of the fleet, intercepted a flotilla of French ships carrying a cargo of portable wooden huts to be used in the invasion of England. As it sailed past Sandwich he captured the ships and sailed triumphantly back into Sandwich harbour where the huts were immediately set up to use as defences.

Also sometime during the year Harry gave evidence in the famous Scrope/Grosvenor trial (Geoffrey Chaucer was also called as a witness) which was concerned with the fact that both parties, Scrope and Grosvenor were in dispute about which of them had the right to wear a particular heraldic device. Harry gave evidence in favour of Lord Scrope who was a distant relative of the Percies. He stated that he was aged 20, had borne arms himself since 1377 at the siege of Berwick, and that he believed Lord Scrope to be in the right. The Earl of Northumberland also gave evidence and for a time he presided over the trial as a judge. After lasting many years the court eventually found in favour of Lord Scrope.

In 1386 when his father re-married, Harry gained a new step-mother, the heiress, Maud Lucy of Cockermouth. Cockermouth castle then came into the hands of the Percies and the Lucy 'fish' (right) were incorporated into the Percy arms. Also sadly late that year or early in 1387 his younger brother, Thomas Percy, died of the plague in Castile where he was serving in John of Gaunt's army. He left a widow and two young children and the wardship of some of their lands fell to his brothers, Harry and Ralph.

Popular idol

In 1387 some of King Richard's favourites at court persuaded the king to send Harry to sea again in anticipation of another raid by the French. These royal favourites were jealous of Harry's popularity so they sent him in a leaking boat in the hope that it would sink. However he returned safely and, much to their chagrin, had won even more honours for the king and was feted more than ever.

A contemporary description of Hotspur described him as *'handsome, tall of stature, a graceful bearing and generally of sweet countenance except when he was in the grip of a moody passion, to which he was prone. He had black curling hair which flowed unchecked beside his cheeks and dark hazel fiery eyes which showed he never lacked courage. He was valiant and chivalrous and was the toast of London because of his youthful good looks and utter fearlessness.'*

He was hailed as a knight in the mould of the Black Prince by the Londoners who tried to emulate his strange manner of speech - which could either have referred to his rough northern burr (the Northumbrian 'R' is sometimes attributed to Hotspur) or the fact that he spoke with a certain hesitation or impediment. Many young lads sought to serve him as a squire or page and wear the Percy crest.

Further honours were heaped on him in the spring of 1388 when he was invested by the King as a knight of the Garter. This meant that three of the Percy family - the Earl, Sir Thomas Percy (the earl's brother) and Harry - were members of the Order of the Garter at the same time which was most unusual.

In June, Harry was appointed Warden of the East March and Berwick for three years but this expired on his capture by the Scots at Otterburn in August.

Berwick Gate

Part III - 1388 - The Battle of Otterburn

The famous Battle of Otterburn took place on Wednesday 12th August 1388 and the chief protagonists were James, Earl of Douglas (born 1358) who was known as Sir James of Liddesdale, and Sir Henry Percy, known as Harry Hotspur, eldest son and heir to the first Earl of Northumberland. The events leading up to the battle fell somewhere between following the usual pattern for a large border raid and preparing for a full-scale war.

The chief earls and barons of Scotland met at Aberdeen and planned a major incursion into England without their king's consent. They arranged for their forces to muster at Jedburgh at the beginning of August and on the appointed day, four earls - Fife, Moray, March and Douglas, along with Sir Archibald (the Grim) Douglas, Sir John Montgomery - with his son and two grandsons, Sir John Maxwell, and various members of the Lindsays, Drummonds, and Soutars came together to plan their tactics.

Crossed Pennants of Percy and Douglas

The Battle Plan

The Scots decided to split their large forces (supposedly around 40,000) because of information received from a captured Englishman. This young man, coming upon a large gathering of Scots as he rode back to Northumberland, had dismounted and tied his horse to a tree in order to creep forward to ascertain the nature of the gathering. Unfortunately, when he went back for his horse, it was missing and he was discovered, while searching for the animal, by the fact that he was still wearing his spurs. Under interrogation he confessed that the Percies already knew of the impending invasion through their spies. Such a large gathering of Scots would have been hard to miss.

Accordingly, the main body of the army marched for Carlisle under the Earl of Fife while the earls of Douglas and Moray were detached with a flying column to harass the Earl of Northumberland.

Scottish Pennants

They thundered through the north of England by way of Reedsmire, Ottercops and Rothley Crags, foraging all the way to Brancepeth on the Yorkshire border where, wearying of the lack of opposition, they wheeled about and marched on Newcastle. Douglas found the town in possession of the two young Percies - Hotspur and his brother, Ralph - who had been sent there in anticipation by their father while he waited in Alnwick to outflank the Scots on their way home.

Newcastle West Gate

The Scottish troops attempted to take the gates of the city but were easily repulsed and three or four days of incessant skirmishing ensued between detachments of both armies outside the walls with single combats between knights. Douglas challenged Hotspur and they fought hand to hand on horseback then, according to some sources, Hotspur's horse stumbled and he fell to the ground where he lay stunned. Before the Scots reacted, several of his squires rushed out of the city and carried him back inside the walls. Douglas captured Hotspur's fallen pennon (which had been forgotten in the rush) and challenged Hotspur to come and get it when he took it back to Scotland to fly on his tower. *"By God,"* Hotspur is reported to have replied, *"you shall never leave Northumberland alive with it."*

"Then you must come and take it this night," answered Douglas, *"Your pennon shall stand before my tent, for him to take who dares!"*

Otterburn

The Scottish army set off for Ponteland which they took and burned and, on the following day, they attacked the tower at Otterburn but were unable to capture it. Then they camped for the night in a wood - Douglas choosing his site, with an eye to attack from archery.

Hotspur, on being reliably informed by his spies that the rest of the Scots army were not likely to launch an attack on his forces when they left Newcastle, set out on that day with 600 spears and 8000 foot and force-marched to Otterburn which they reached late in the evening, after the Scots had finished eating and were resting for the night. Although it was bright moonlight, Hotspur's troops mistook the Scots picket lines and baggage train for the main force and attacked, thus giving the Scottish knights time to rally and fall upon the English flank. Hotspur almost captured Douglas's banner and only the gallantry of Sir Patrick Hepburn and his son saved it.

The Scots began giving way under pressure of numbers and Douglas thrust forward to try and regain lost ground. Unfortunately, as his armour had been hastily thrown on and was not fastened properly, he was only able to deliver blows, not parry them and so fell, wounded in the shoulder, stomach and thigh by three spears. As he fell his own great battle axe gashed his skull. Some Scottish sources say that, due to the crush of the press and the foresight of his squires, who bore him on shouting their battle cry 'A Douglas! A Douglas!', the Scots (who would otherwise have routed at the death of their

Douglas Banner

leader) were kept unaware of his fate. Other sources state that his body lay undiscovered until the next day[1].

Meanwhile Ralph Percy, like Douglas, had pressed too far forward into the enemy, was surrounded and fell, badly wounded in front of Sir John Maxwell, who was fighting in the Earl of Moray's wing. When Ralph was invited to surrender he asked Maxwell for permission to empty his greaves of blood before handing over his sword. Hotspur, attempting to reach his fallen brother was taken prisoner by Lord Montgomery and the two Percies were held to ransom for £3000, £1000 of which was paid in two instalments by the king and council of England - one paid at Easter 1389 and the other at Michaelmas (29th September) 1390.

The cause of the English defeat was put down to the fact that they were overtaxed by their forced march from Newcastle followed by a battle lasting through the entire night - local sources say that skirmishes continued for two or three days afterwards. Once the two Percies were taken, the English forces were driven back and became entangled with the Bishop of Durham's troops who were hurrying to the battle with reinforcements, unfortunately too late to make an impact but an unusual incident took place in this melee.

Sir Matthew Redman, Governor of Berwick, was retreating from the field when he was singled out by Sir James Lindsay who reckoned that he must be very important due to the 'beauty of his armour'. After being pursued for three miles, Redman found his horse so fatigued it was impossible to go on so he dismounted and bravely awaited his pursuer. Lindsay also alighted and a fierce conflict commenced between the two knights, until the Scotsman eventually prevailed. Redman surrendered and, as was common practice at the time, obtained leave to depart, giving his oath that he would return as Lindsay's prisoner in twenty days. This was accepted in the knowledge that violation of an oath was too infamous to even consider. Lindsay let his prisoner go and, on his way to join the rest of his countrymen, rode straight into a body of men led by the Bishop of Durham. It was his turn to be taken prisoner and he was carried to Newcastle where Redman recognised him and insisted on his release. Scottish chroniclers report that Redman set him free but, unless it was on the same understanding as his own conditions of capture, this is incorrect. On the 25th September at the Cambridge parliament, an order was issued by King

---

[1] For a plan of the battle, see
http://www.battlefieldsofbritain.co.uk/battle_otterburn_1381.html

Richard to the Earl of Northumberland 'not to dismiss Sir James Lindsay who had been lately made a prisoner, either for pledge or ransom, until he received further orders from the king and his said council'.

Victory was ultimately accredited to the Scots, despite the fact that their leader had been killed. English losses were given as 3000 slain, wounded or taken prisoner, while the Scots only lost 300. The battle of Otterburn is still a matter for debate in some quarters along the Borders, as is Hotspur's captured pennon. Some claim it remains in the hands of the Douglases of Cavers, along with a glove embroidered with the Percy crescent and the initials 'H.P.' - supposedly a lady's favour carried by Hotspur but, although this was reputedly seen around the seventeenth century, there is no evidence to substantiate it.

Hotspur's captivity

According to Hardyng's Chronicle[2] Harry Hotspur was imprisoned at Dunbar after Otterburn. Some Scottish sources indicate that there was great discussion as to what to do with the Percies. The Douglas family, among others, were all for killing Hotspur to avenge the death of the Earl of Douglas. (People were saying that Hotspur had killed the Earl, though some Scots believed it might have been treachery by one of their own side with a personal grievance.) The Scottish Earl of March 'greatly feared' a rescue attempt by the Northumbrians and incarcerated him in his stronghold of Dunbar until the ransom was found.

Dunbar Castle

---

[2] John Hardyng, the fourteenth century chronicler, joined Hotspur's household in 1390 as a twelve-year-old page.

Ralph Percy was allowed home when only part of the money had been paid on account of his serious wounds. This was in the Scots own interest for, if he had died in captivity, there would have been no need to pay the remainder whereas if he died at home the Percies were still duty bound to honour the ransom.

It is believed that Harry was released only when the full amount had been paid towards the end of September 1390 although he may have been freed slightly earlier as he was re-appointed as Warden of the West March and Carlisle in June of that year.

Also around this time Hotspur became the guardian of the infant Gilbert Umfraville on the death of his father, Sir Thomas Umfraville of Harbottle Castle who, with his brother Robert, led the attack on the Scots camp at the Battle of Otterburn. Later in life, as Sir Gilbert of Kyme, this young man served under King Henry V in France where he was noted for his martial skills, no doubt acquired from his early training by Hotspur.

A rather strange footnote to the battle of Otterburn occurred in 1389. Archibald (the Grim), succeeded his brother and as third Earl of Douglas marched over the Border in the late summer to 'beat up the quarters' of King Richard's new Warden of the Eastern Marches, Sir Thomas Mowbray, Earl Marshall of England who had been appointed in June 1389 in Hotspur's absence. Seemingly the Earl Marshall was reported to have spoken contemptuously of the performance of the Percies at Otterburn and the Scots saw this as a reflection on their own honour and prowess.

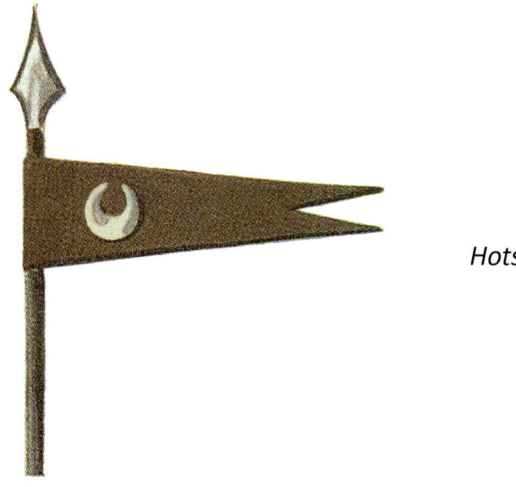

Hotspur's Pennon

Part IV - 1390-1399 - Expeditions Abroad

Towards the end of 1390 Hotspur commanded a second expedition to raise the siege of Brest, in France, and while he was away his brother, Ralph, distinguished himself in the defence of the Western Marches. The area had been invaded by a party of Scots who took advantage of the absence of both Hotspur and the Earl of Northumberland (who was Governor of Calais at the time).

The following year, 1391, Harry took part in a tournament at St Inglevert, near Calais, which attracted the foremost knights of Europe. Over sixty knights and squires (known as 'the flower of England') set sail in March to take part in the Jousts. Harry rode in the company of his half-cousin, Henry Bolingbroke, the future King Henry IV. The colourful scene, with its fluttering banners, coats of arms and heralds, centred on three vermilion tents - one for each of the three renowned French challengers. In front of each tent was a white shield and a black (the white shield of peace signified combat with blunted weapons and the black shield of war indicated combat with sharpened weapons).

In order to engage battle each knight sent his squire to strike the appropriate shield and it was noted that most of the young Englishmen chose the dangerous option, aquitting themselves well.

Teutonic Knights

Harry Hotspur and Henry Bolingbroke were the acknowledged English champions and, in consequence of this, they were invited by the Teutonic Knights to join one of their crusades to Prussia and Lithuania against the 'heathen hordes' who populated these lands and were reputed to be 'cruel and savage fighters who refused to embrace christianity' and fiercely resisted the culture of western Europe.

Harry returned home to prepare for the campaign then joined Bolingbroke, a seasoned campaigner who went on regular expeditions and always travelled with a great retinue which included household musicians (trumpeters, drummers and pipers) and he sent heralds on ahead to announce his coming, distributing alms to the people when he arrived. They set sail in July from Boston in Lincolnshire for Ruischift in Northern Germany where Bolingbroke and some of his party (presumably including Hotspur) disembarked to travel overland, while the rest continued by sea to Konigsberg, a major Hanseatic port on the

Konigsburg Castle and Cathedral

Baltic where the German kings were crowned. The whole event took on the semblance of a holiday for, when all the knights were assembled, feasting took place for ten days and the Grand Master of the Teutonic Knights gave a magnificent banquet in the hall at Konigsberg where the visiting knights were seated at a table of honour. The cause of the crusade was proclaimed and preparations began the next day to embark on the expedition.

After a very successful campaign in which Bolingbroke and Harry helped the Teutonic Knights win two victories, and a pleasant winter spent entertaining in rented Prussian castles the party returned in April 1392 to a rapturous reception in Hull. [Note: When Bolingbroke offered to aid the Teutonic knights again in Lithuania during his exile in 1398/9, his offer was turned down and 'one of the sons of Earl Percy' (presumably Harry) was also turned away in the mid 1390s.]

Diplomatic Service

Also in 1392 Harry accompanied his uncle, Sir Thomas Percy, the English Ambassador to France and Spain, on a diplomatic visit to France to discuss the French desire to reclaim Aquitaine - a part of France which had belonged to England since Eleanor of Aquitaine married King Henry II. John of Gaunt, who was currently styled as Prince of Aquitaine and Gascony, accompanied by his son, Henry Bolingbroke, spearheaded the mission by royal command.

Hotspur was sent on another diplomatic mission on behalf of the king in 1393 when he met King James of Cyprus who sent a glowing letter of thanks to Richard for having sent him so gracious an ambassador.

"Nicossea. July 15th 1393.

And on this (latter) my dear brother, it concerned you that (in the matter of) your noble relative, Lord Henry Percy, that we afford him respect and honour (and of which you thank us again); he himself said of his respect and honour that he was pleased, but we would maintain that in visiting us he has given us the greater honour and we offer him many thanks."

From 1393 to March 1394 Hotspur was appointed as Governor of Bordeaux but was refused admittance to the town until he had succeeded in convincing the authorities that he came as a direct representative of King Richard and not from John of Gaunt, whose nomination as Prince of Aquitaine and Gascony was resented so badly by the locals that they refused to acknowledge him.

In 1394 Harry's first child was born. He had a son, Henry, by Elizabeth Mortimer, granddaughter of Lionel, Duke of Clarence (the brother of the Black Prince, and half-cousin to both King Richard and Henry Bolingbroke). Elizabeth's brother, Roger Mortimer, was named as heir to the throne by the childless Richard. Elizabeth was born at Usk on 12th February 1371 or 1372 and baptised by William Courtnay, Bishop of Hereford on 16th February but it is not known when or where Elizabeth and Harry were married.

Bordeaux Gate

It is likely that Elizabeth moved to Alnwick around 1383 when she became a ward of Earl Percy and betrothed to his eldest son, but it seems that she and Harry did not live together as man and wife until after his imprisonment in Scotland. They had a daughter, Elizabeth, who later married her cousin, Ralph Neville, second Earl of Westmorland. In 1395 Hotspur was appointed Governor of Berwick.

During 1396 Hotspur made a final trip to France, once again in the retinue of his uncle, Sir Thomas Percy, to bring back the new Queen Isabel, daughter of King Charles of France, who married King Richard in a splendid ceremony at Calais on All Hallows. It is possible that Elizabeth accompanied Harry since Isabel was only eight years old. The Queen's coronation took place in Westminster Abbey at Christmas and Harry and his brother, Ralph, took part in the magnificent international tournament at Smithfield where he performed with his usual skill and held the field against all comers. Once more, he and Henry Bolingbroke both excelled individually.

In 1397 Hotspur and his father were requested in a letter from Bolingbroke not to interfere in a dispute between three Northumbrians - Sir Henry Heton versus William Swinburne and John Fenwick, all of whom were knights banneret to the Earl of Northumberland. The dispute had arisen over the possession of the Heton estates and Swinburne, who was retained for an yearly annuity by Bolingbroke's father, John of Gaunt, had appealed to the House of Lancaster. It is likely that Heton had approached the Percies to plead his case for him but the eventual outcome of the case is unknown.

In 1398 Harry's brother, Ralph, set off on a pilgrimage to the Holy Land. Originally Henry Bolingbroke led the party but he turned back at Rhodes while the others continued to make for Jerusalem where Ralph was killed in 1399 in action against the Saracens.

Percy Lion, emblem of the Percy family, symbolising courage and strength.

The Percy motto is 'Esperance en Dieu' - Hope in God.

Part V - 1399 - Bolingbroke's Rebellion

Henry Bolingbroke fell out of favour with King Richard in 1399 and he and Thomas Mowbray were sentenced to banishment for supposed treason - Mowbray for life and Bolingbroke for ten years, later commuted to six on account of John of Gaunt, the king's uncle, pleading for his son. On the eve of Bolingbroke's embarkation to France, Hotspur accompanied his father at the head of a large number of knights and squires to see him off, as a demonstration that they were all displeased with the king for banishing him.

A few months later, when John of Gaunt died, Richard changed Bolingbroke's sentence to exile for life and confiscated his Lancaster inheritance. The Earl of Northumberland and Hotspur vainly argued with the king on behalf of their kinsman (the Earl was cousin to Bolingbroke's mother, Blanche of Lancaster). They then left court and retired to the north where Hotspur spoke out against the king, accusing him of 'governing foolishly under the influence of evil counsellors'. On hearing of this, Richard summoned the Percies back to London where his advisors were suggesting he 'collect them by prison or otherwise' but Thomas Percy, the Earl's brother, warned them not to trust themselves into the king's power or their lives would be in jeopardy. The Earl pleaded that the state of the Borders did not permit them to present themselves at court and Richard passed sentence of banishment and confiscation on them in their absence. When this was published throughout the towns and cities of England, the Londoners 'greatly marvelled and could not know for what cause it was; for the Earl and his son were valiant men' and the Scottish king offered them sanctuary. Harry and his father however preferred to remain secure in their own territories in Northumberland.

Lancaster Arms - adopted by Henry Bolingbroke on the death of his father, John of Gaunt

Bolingbroke's Rebellion

King Richard embarked for Ireland, with Thomas Percy as commander-in-chief of the fleet on a punitive expedition to avenge the death of the Governor of Ireland and heir to the throne, Roger Mortimer (Hotspur's brother in law), who had been killed in an ambush by the 'wild Irish'. While the king was away, Henry Bolingbroke landed at Ravenspur on the Yorkshire coast with a few friends and fellow exiles and Hotspur rode to join them.

They marched through the Lancaster lands in North Yorkshire to Pontefract where they were met by the Earls of Northumberland, Henry Percy, and Westmorland, Ralph Neville who was Harry's maternal uncle. Bolingbroke swore a most sacred oath on the body and blood of Christ that he had come to claim only that which was his by right, the Lancaster inheritance, and he appointed Harry's father Earl Marshall of the troops.

Soon most of the country had defected to Bolingbroke, including the Duke of York, the only surviving son of King Edward III and uncle to Richard and Bolingbroke, who had been left in charge of England while the king was away.

On Richard's return he sought refuge in Conwy Castle in Wales and instructed Sir Thomas Percy, in his capacity as Steward of England, to dismiss the household after which Thomas 'broke his staff of office', resigned his commission and joined his brother and Hotspur in Bolingbroke's army.

The Percies featured largely in the forced abdication of King Richard. The Earl of Northumberland, with Bishop Arundel, met with Richard at Conwy and persuaded him to come out and meet Henry at Flint Castle, the Earl swearing a sacred oath on the Chalice (as Bolingbroke had at Pontefract) that Richard would not be harmed. Hotspur, commanding the 80,000 army, came with Sir Thomas Percy and Henry Bolingbroke from Chester to Flint. On reaching Flint castle, Bolingbroke met the king and

Coronation of Henry IV

dismissed 60,000 troops - including those of Hotspur, Northumberland and Westmorland - retaining 20,000 of his own men to conduct Richard to London where he was incarcerated in the Tower of London until he agreed to abdicate.

Some sources state that the Percies took a leading part in the deposition of King Richard in the hope that Bolingbroke would rule as regent for the six year old heir to the throne, Edmund Mortimer - Elizabeth Percy's nephew, until he came of age. Others believe it was for personal aggrandisement for, when Bolingbroke took the throne, as King Henry IV, they were rewarded by being reinstated into their former positions.

On the eve of Henry's coronation the Earl of Northumberland was invested as Constable of England and granted lordship of the Isle of Man. Harry was appointed as Sheriff of Northumberland and confirmed as Constable of Berwick and the East Marches (he had been removed from office by Richard for treasonable language). He became Constable of Roxburgh - though Henry shortly passed this to Ralph Neville, Earl of Westmorland - and was granted for life the Castle and lordship of Bamburgh which was part of the Lancaster inheritance.

Bamburgh Castle

He became Justiciary of Chester, North Wales and Flintshire and was granted Beaumaris and Anglesey for life, the restoration of his wife's Mortimer inheritance. This was later given to the Prince of Wales on attaining his fifteenth year. The council did suggest that Hotspur could be recompensed for the loss from Sir Edmund Mortimer's lands but he declined as Mortimer was Elizabeth's brother and he 'refused to be enriched at the cost of a kinsman'.

Although the Percies were employed by Henry to watch the Borders of Scotland and North Wales they had to do so largely out of their own pockets as Henry was virtually bankrupt. On 1st March 1402, for example, he had to borrow £40 for expenses 'attendant upon his daughter's wedding'. One of the reasons for King Henry's insolvency seems to have been caused by the fall in price of customs on wool which was a chief source of revenue to the Crown. In Richard's reign the price had been £46,000 per annum but this fell to £20,000 in 1402. Henry IV's annual income was less than £90,000 whereas previous monarchs had averaged £116,000 at least.

Alnwick Castle Keep

Part VI - 1400-1402 - Scotland and Wales

Scotland

Around the turn of the year Hotspur figured in the conclusion to a Treaty of Amity (friendship) between the king and George Dunbar, the Scottish Earl of March. March had left Scotland on account of his quarrel with the Scottish king who had slighted March's daughter by annulling her marriage to his son in favour of the daughter of the powerful Douglas family. Dunbar swore fealty to the English king and Hotspur petitioned for safe conduct and grazing over many miles of meadows near Caldbrandspeth of two flocks of 1600 sheep belonging to the Countess of March and her sister.

Hailes Castle

In Spring 1400 Hotspur accompanied the Scottish Earl of March on a raid of reprisal into East Lothian as far as Popple, burning the villages of Hailes, Traprain and Markle. They unsuccessfully assaulted Hailes castle but were forced to withdraw upon the appearance of the Master of Douglas, Sir Archibald the Grim, with a Scots army who pursued them back to Berwick.

In August of the same year Harry and his father accompanied King Henry on another futile expedition into Scotland to try and force the Scottish king to pay homage to the English crown.

Wales

Later in the year Hotspur was appointed guardian and tutor to the Prince of Wales, the thirteen year old heir to the throne and future King Henry V. It was partly due to Hotspur's excellent instruction that the young Prince Hal learned the art of soldiery for which he later became famous at Agincourt and which, in the meantime, stood him in good stead as he and Hotspur struggled to hold the Welsh border during the uprising of Owen Glendower.

Glendower was a well-educated Welsh nobleman who had read law at the Inns of Court in London. He had been in dispute over land with Lord Grey of Ruthin, a good friend of King Henry IV. Grey had failed to issue a call to arms to Glendower during the Scottish expedition earlier in the year and the Welshman had been declared a traitor in his absence. On 16th September Glendower proclaimed himself Prince of Wales and sacked the lands of Ruthin, burning and pillaging as far as Shropshire before being driven off and taking to the Welsh hills.

In October the king led a punitive expedition into Wales, leaving Prince Hal at Chester with his council, headed by Hotspur whom the chronicler, Adam of Usk, described as 'the flower and glory of the chivalry of Christendom'.

Conwy Castle

On 1st April 1401, Good Friday, Conwy Castle in Wales was seized by William and Rhys Tudor while the garrison of fifteen men at arms and sixty lances were at Mass. The Tudors' forces gained entrance by planting one of their supporters inside in the guise of a carpenter - Glendower had a good many tacit sympathisers, including the abbot of Conwy. Harry and Prince Hal recaptured the castle at the end of May after a siege and a pardon was offered to the Tudors on condition that nine of the worst offenders surrendered. As none were willing to volunteer this was achieved by the Welsh seizing the unfortunate nine men as they slept and handing them over for execution. The nine were promptly hung, drawn and quartered in a particularly gory fashion

Conwy Castle

to dissuade any other would-be offenders against English 'justice'. During the siege Hotspur was awarded £200 back payment on 19th April to defer expenses he had met from his own purse to pay his troops but this was never paid.

In June, Harry, while marching from Denbigh, routed the Welsh in an engagement at Cader Idris in a pincer movement with John Charlton, Lord of Powys who attacked the retreating Welsh and captured part of Glendower's personal armour.

Between 10th April and 3rd July Harry sent five letters to the king from Denbigh, Carnarvon and Swynshede begging for monetary assistance for his soldiers on both Marches (Wales and the North). The following extract, written from Carnarvon on 2nd May, contains the substance of all of them. *"Remember how I have repeatedly applied for payment of the king's troops at Berwick in the East March of England, who are in such distress as they can no longer bear or endure for want of money; and I therefore implore you to order that they might be paid as was agreed upon between the treasurer and myself at our last meeting, if better means cannot be adopted, as otherwise I shall have to go to you in person to claim payment to the neglect of other duties."*

Shortly after this Harry resigned his commission due to continuing inability to pay his men, no money being forthcoming from King or council. He returned to the northern borders while his uncle, Sir Thomas Percy, took over the Prince's guardianship.

In November 1401 Owen Glendower contacted Hotspur to ask the king for a pardon and was told that if he submitted, the Earl of Northumberland and Harry would plead his cause before the king. He replied that, having seen what parliament did to others in 1400, he did not dare for fear of his life. Hotspur is supposed to have interviewed him to discover his exact requirements. These were: a royal pardon, some evidence of the king's goodwill, and three months armistice. When Harry brought this to the council some of the councillors advocated continuing negotiations while plotting to murder Glendower, to which Hotspur replied that it was not in keeping with his rank to use the oath of fealty as a means of deception. The council decided 'it neither was, nor could be, honourable and befitting the king's majesty to remit such a malefactor his offence' and the uprising continued.

Family note: Around this time Hotspur's sister, Margaret, is believed to have married Sir Alan Fenwick (of Fenwick, Matfen, Cambo and Hartington). Fenwick's mother was Elizabeth Heton, heiress of the Heton lands of Lowick and Ingram. A son was born to them on Christmas Day 1401 at Alnwick Castle and the child was baptised at Alnwick church the next day and named Henry. His godparents were the Earl of Northumberland and Sir Henry Percy of Atholl (the son of Harry's brother, Thomas, who had died in 1386). The earl's brother, Sir Thomas Percy, was also present and gave the infant 40s and his nurse 6s 8d 'for the joy of his birth'. A lighted torch was carried in front of the baby from the castle to the church and was held before him at his baptism. When Hotspur's son, Sir Henry Percy, was restored to the earldom of Northumberland under Henry V, he appointed Sir Henry Fenwick (presumed to be his cousin) as sheriff of Northumberland.

Alnwick Castle through the Percy crest

Part VII - 1402 - The Battle of Homildon

The Battle of Homildon

During 1402 Hotspur was kept busy in Northumberland in his capacity as Warden of the Marches. Early in the year a succession of short-lived peace treaties with the Scots finally came to an end and they resumed their raids across the border. In Spring, Thomas Haliburton, a lowland lord, led a successful foray into the countryside around Bamburgh and returned with great spoils. Another raiding party, led by the young Patrick Hepburn of Hailes, was returning laden with plunder on 7th May when they were surprised on Nesbitt Moor by an equal number of English, under the command of George Dunbar and his son. Thousands of the Scots 'the flower of the youth of Lothian' were slain and many of their captains (including Hepburn and Haliburton) fell into Hotspur's hands to be ransomed as he saw fit.

In August, the Earl of Douglas, wishing to avenge the Scottish losses, led an army of reprisal deep into England, penetrating as far as the river Wear. On their return they found their passage to Scotland blocked near Milfield by Hotspur, with his father and Earl Dunbar, at the head of a large army. On the morning of 14th September the Scots halted at Humbleton (Homildon) Hill, near Wooler, while the Northumbrian forces seized the opposite hill and barred their way forward. Hotspur, in command of the advance, was all for rushing up the hill to attack the Scots but Dunbar, a wily general with knowledge of Scots tactics, held onto the bridle of Hotspur's horse and advised him to employ the English archers in the valley between the two armies.

Scottish defeat

The Scots forces, numbering about 12,000, included 30 French knights of distinction as well as Murdoch Stewart, Earl of Fife, a close relative

View from Humbleton Hill

of the Scottish king and the Earl of Douglas at their head. The first hundred Scots fell under the lethal hail of arrows before three Scottish knights attempted to cut their way through but they were soon killed or captured and their men utterly routed. The five remaining Scottish earls: Fife, Angus, Moray, Orkney and Douglas himself (who was wounded in five places and lost an eye) were taken prisoner and such was the general panic that 500 fugitives were drowned miles away in the river Tweed as they tried to reach Scotland. The English victory was so complete that their men-at-arms were never even called into action and the main battle was over within an hour.[1] The news was swiftly taken to King Henry by one of Hotspur's squires who was well rewarded by the king.

The only unchivalrous deed ever accorded to Hotspur took place after this battle. Sir William Stewart of Teviotdale and his squire, Thomas Ker were among the captives and Hotspur argued that, as Teviotdale was at that time in English hands, they should be regarded as traitors. Stewart was a very eloquent speaker and managed to convince three successive juries that they should be aquitted but Hotspur appointed a new jury, made up of his own followers, who pronounced them guilty and they were hung, drawn and quartered.

Confrontation with the king

On September 22nd 1402 a proclamation was issued by King Henry forbidding the Percies to ransom or exchange the prisoners they had taken at Homildon and commanding them to bring the Scottish lords to London. Although the king assured them that they should not be the losers by this change in Border policy, both the Northumbrians and the Scots were infuriated by this breach of border custom, as normally this was one of the ways in which the Marcher Lords paid their soldiers and gave the enemy a chance to return to their homes as soon as possible. King Henry apparently felt he could secure a more lasting peace with Scotland if the foremost earls were held hostage in England so, on 20th October, the Earl of Northumberland brought Murdoch Stewart with his fellow countrymen and the French knights in triumph to London. Hotspur, however, remained in the north on the excuse that Earl Douglas was unfit to travel because of his wounds.

King Henry remained seated on his throne in Parliament House to receive the captives and expressed anger over the fact that Hotspur and Douglas were

---

[1] For a plan of the battle see
http://www.battlefieldsofbritain.co.uk/battle_homildon_hill_1402.html

Henry IV and Advisors

absent. Northumberland and the king exchanged heated words over the border expenses which had been incurred by the Percies in the king's service and Henry, who had spent all his funds earlier in the year on his marriage to Joan of Navarre, told the Earl that he had no money and demanded Hotspur's immediate attendance with his prisoner.

Hotspur duly arrived alone and, during an audience with Henry, suggested that Douglas be exchanged for his brother-in-law, Edmund Mortimer, who was held by Owen Glendower in Wales. Glendower had captured Mortimer (Elizabeth Percy's brother) on 22nd June in a foray near Knighton in which the Welsh archers in the English forces turned against their commanders. The Percies were annoyed at the government's slowness to ransom him - as opposed to the swift ransom of Sir Reginald Grey of Ruthin who had been taken prisoner by the Welsh in April and ransomed almost immediately.

King Henry declared Mortimer a traitor for allowing himself to be captured in such suspicious circumstances and stated that public money would not be spent on strengthening his enemies. Hotspur called him to task. *"How is this? You would have us expose ourselves when your crown is in danger and yet you will not help us."* The king lost his temper and accused Harry of also being a traitor - which he vehemently denied - and Henry in exasperation drew his dagger on him. At this, Hotspur flung down his gage in a knightly challenge and declared *"Not here but in the field"* before departing without leave for the North.

Mortimer, despairing of being ransomed, at the end of November married Glendower's daughter and placed his lands in Wales at the rebels' disposal.

On 7th December Hotspur sent into the Exchequer of Receipt eight tallies amounting to £4,115 which he had been unable to cash with the accountants to whom they were presented. He had been trying unsuccessfully to realise these tallies for expenses since 13th March and found the council less than helpful. According to some sources, certain members of the king's council were ill-disposed towards Hotspur because of his popularity with the people.

Early in 1403 a dispute arose between the vassals of the Earl of Westmorland and those of the Percies regarding their rights to prisoners taken at Homildon. Westmorland appealed to the king to appoint Lord Lovel and eight others to look into the case as, although normally it should have been judged in one of the Border courts, both the Earl of Northumberland and Hotspur had a vested interest in the outcome and could not be relied upon to come to an independent judgement. The outcome of the affair is unknown.

Hotspur's Personal Shield - the blue Percy lion on a gold background cut by red bars depicting the eldest son

Part VIII - 1403 - The Battle of Shrewsbury

On 2nd March 1403 King Henry declared that the greater part of southern Scotland had been conquered and was now annexed to England. At the same time he conferred the lands belonging to the Earl of Douglas - the country between the river Tweed and the Border, and the greater part of Galloway - on the Percies, providing they could subdue them, in lieu of payment.

Hotspur immediately set about consolidating the English gains on the Borders but was unable to overcome Cocklaw Tower at Ormiston, near Hawick so, after a short siege, in May both parties agreed on a suspension of hostilities on provision that the garrison would surrender on 1st August if not relieved by the Scottish government.

On 30th May the Earl of Northumberland wrote to the Privy Council in London informing them that he and his son had bound themselves by an indenture to be at Ormiston on 1st August to receive possession of the castle if it had not been rescued by battle. He also asked them to implore the king for further funds so that he and Hotspur would know by 24th June if they could rely on support. The king responded initially by informing the Earl that he considered the Percies to be sufficiently strong to overcome Scots opposition at Ormiston without help but that a sum of money would be sent as soon as possible. Northumberland replied by return that they needed £20,000 as the balance of arrears owed to them. King Henry, unable to find the money, set off north in early July to assist them with his own forces.

Hotspur's Arms

While he was on his way Henry discovered that Hotspur, with the Earl of Douglas, was already on the march south towards Shrewsbury to meet up with his brother-in-law, Edmund Mortimer, and the army of Glendower. Hotspur stopped at Chester, making his headquarters in the house of Dame Petronilla Clark, where he was met by his uncle, Sir Thomas Percy, Earl of Worcester, bearing a document drawn up by him and Harry's father accusing the king of obtaining the crown by fraud and using money raised by taxation for his private purse instead of for the defence of the nation. Some sources also state that the Earl of Northumberland had sent out letters to other great lords asking them for support, to which they all replied in the affirmative except for the Earl of Stafford - though few of them kept their word. These letters were entrusted to Hotspur's squire, John Hardyng, who had fought under him at Homildon and Ormiston.

The king heard of the rebellion at Leicester and on 16th July, from Burton on Trent, issued a command to all sheriffs of the Midland counties to join him with all available forces. He then set off immediately for Shrewsbury where the young Prince of Wales commanded the garrison.

Centre: Hotspur

Left: Sir Thomas Percy

Right: The Earl of Douglas

Centre: King Henry IV

Left: The Earl of Dunbar

Right: The Earl of Stafford

Hotspur waited until he heard that Glendower and Mortimer were on the march before leaving Chester and was disconcerted to find that Henry had reached Shrewsbury before him on 20th July.

Hotspur decided to withdraw along the Whitchurch road to a strong position on the slope of Haytely field in the parish of Allbright Hussey.

Shields of the Protagonists

Shields of the Knights serving with HOTSPUR'S ARMY

Shields of the Knights serving with the KING'S ARMY

The front of his force was protected by a tangled crop of peas and three small ponds, while his right was flanked by the river Severn and the rear by steep ground. Although Glendower's scouts were in view, there was no sign of Mortimer and Glendower, or the Earl of Northumberland who had been taken ill at Berwick upon Tweed.

The Battle of Shrewsbury

The following day the king's army advanced to the foot of the slope and divided into three sections - the centre being commanded by King Henry himself, the left flank by the Prince of Wales and the right by the Earl of Stafford. Hotspur sent two squires, Thomas Knayton and Roger Salome, to the king with a document of indictment which had been drawn up by his uncle, the Earl of Worcester, and the Earl of Northumberland accusing Henry of various charges including:

1) being false and foresworn in breaking a binding oath that he had only come to claim his rights as Duke of Lancaster;

2) causing King Richard to be starved to death;

3) levying taxes without Parliament's consent;

4) usurping the throne - excluding the rightful heir and refusing to ransom the heir's closest kinsman when he was taken prisoner in the king's service;

5) accusing those who tried to ransom the heir of treason.

After some protracted parleying - through the Abbot of Shrewsbury for the king and Thomas Percy for Hotspur - impasse was reached as Hotspur was unable to believe that the king's desire for a peaceful settlement was genuine.

"I put no trust in your grace" was his response, to which Henry replied *"I pray the Lord that I may not be held responsible for the blood shed this day"*.

Hotspur had reckoned on engaging the king's forces on 23rd July (after the arrival of Glendower and his troops) but, seeing battle was imminent, he drew up his army in formation and called for the sword he had worn at Homildon, only to be told it had been left behind in the nearby village of Berwick. At this he paled and said *"Now I see my ploughshare is drawing to its last furrow."*

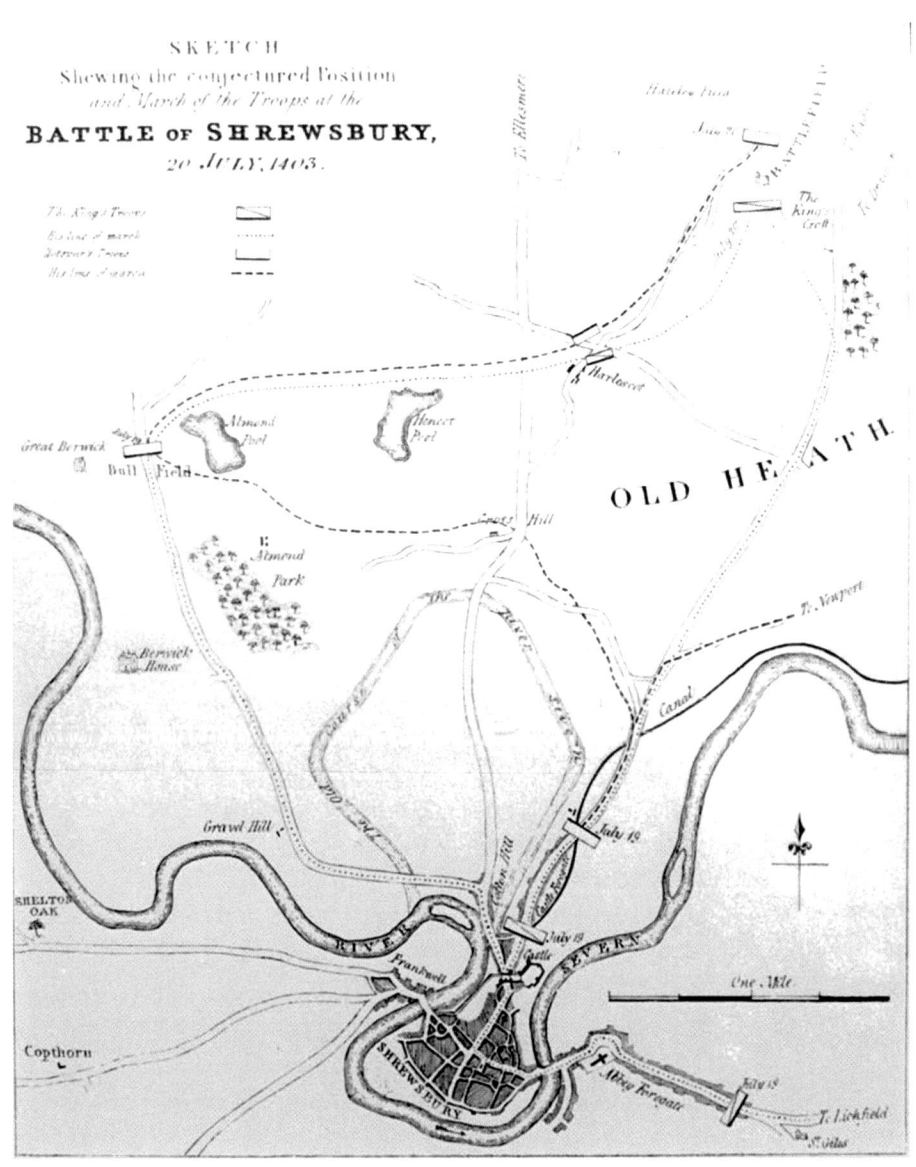

The Battle of Shrewsbury

A soothsayer told me in my own country that I should perish at Berwick. Alas he deceived me by that name which I believed to mean Berwick in the north." He then turned to his army and addressed them much more soberly than his usual enthusiastic manner: *"This day will be a glorious one for us all if we conquer, or will set us free if we are defeated. For it is better to fall on the battlefield in the course of the common weal than after a battle to die by the sentence of our enemies."*

It was midday on Saturday 21st July when the royalist army met the rebels, reputedly numbering 14,000 and including many seasoned soldiers as well as the late King Richard's Cheshire archers. The outcome of the day hung for a long time in the balance and for a while Hotspur's forces held the upper hand.

King Henry set his men uphill towards his opponents on a dangerously narrow front and the bowmen shot into them at short range, wreaking havoc. A contemporary chronicler described it as 'men fell on the king's side as fast as leaves fall in autumn after a hoar frost.' As they advanced the Prince of Wales was wounded in the face but refused to retire, believing that his men might lose heart if he did so.

At one point Hotspur, at the head of a band of about thirty men, cut his way through to the royal standard and almost captured it but the Earl of Stafford seized the banner from the fallen standard bearer and carried it out of the press though he was killed along with many others of the king's men as they ran for their lives. The king himself withdrew to the rear of his forces on the advice of George Dunbar, his wily Scottish ally. The Earl of Douglas, fighting at Hotspur's side - having been promised the town of Berwick upon Tweed as well as the restoration of his lands on the favourable outcome of the battle - distinguished himself with his mighty battle axe and twice or thrice he and Hotspur believed they had killed the king, but each time it was a knight wearing one of the royal suits of armour.

Hotspur's death

The battle raged for five hours until disaster overtook the rebel forces when Henry's reserves joined the flagging royal army and Hotspur, lifting his visor for a moment, was struck by an arrow in the brain and fell dead. Cries of 'Esperance Percy' were drowned by the shout 'Harry Percy is dead' and gradually the rebels were driven back and prisoners taken - the most notable being Thomas Percy, Earl of Worcester and Earl Douglas, who reputedly tried to escape on horseback but was thrown and suffered a broken leg. One chronicler reported that after five hours fighting in the hot sun among dust and the steam rising from sweaty bodies, both sides sank to the ground exhausted, unsure of who had won the battle. Sir Thomas Percy was beheaded and his head displayed on London Bridge and the Earl of Douglas was incarcerated in the Tower of London .

A buckler (shield) was found on the Battlefield which some believe belonged to Hotspur[1]

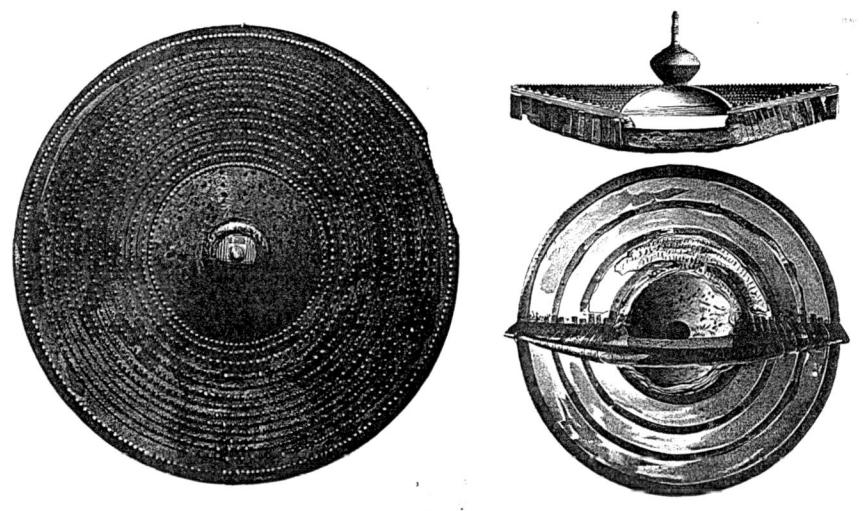

The buckler found on the battlefield

Hotspur's body, which was at first decently laid to rest in a local church, was exhumed the following day, rubbed in salt and hung between two millstones near the pillory in Shrewsbury. King Henry is reputed to have wept over the body of his former friend and relative and he ordered a chantry to be built on the site of the battlefield for prayers for the souls of the dead.

---

[1] The buckler found on the battlefield near Shrewsbury is now housed in Alnwick Castle. It measures thirteen and a half inches in diameter; the convex spiked umbo, within which is the handle, is five inches in diameter. The spike extends three and a half inches beyond its base. The buckler is formed of several layers of stout leather, strongly compacted together by means of brass rivets, passing through narrow concentric bands of iron, thus forming a framework over the entire surface which is slightly concave. There are fourteen rows of rivets. Bucklers of this fashion are rare.

Battlefield Church erected near the site of the battle

Glendower's army never materialised and the Earl of Northumberland, hastening to Hotspur's assistance, was turned back in Yorkshire by the Earl of Westmorland's troops and retreated to Newcastle where only he and his personal retinue were allowed entrance. On hearing the news of his son's death he withdrew to Warkworth castle until summoned by the king to meet him at York. A warrant was also issued for Elizabeth Percy's arrest and delivered by Robert Waterton but there is no record of her being imprisoned.

Hotspur's body was quartered and displayed - the head on Micklegate Bar (the northward facing gate) in York, and the limbs on London Bridge and the gates of Shrewsbury, Chester, and Newcastle upon Tyne - but permission was eventually granted to Lady Percy to gather the remains of her husband for burial. The actual burial place is unknown though traditionally Hotspur's grave is believed to have been on the right side of the high altar in York Minster though some believe his remains were interred in Beverley.

Memorial

Harry Hotspur was known as a 'peerless knight' - a brave and brilliant fighter and a fearless opponent in battle. He was, by profession, a mercenary soldier who earned his salary from the king, or whoever commissioned him, by using his war-like skills to their greatest advantage. He was revered by his contemporaries as a knight in the mould of the Black Prince, whose victories at Crecy and Poitiers were sung for generations, and Henry V, renowned victor of Agincourt, served his apprenticeship in soldiery under Hotspur.

Harry was not a particularly skilful general, rather his personal prowess, both in tournaments and in battle, singled him out and evoked fierce loyalty in his followers and the respect of his enemies. In the barbarous times of the Hundred Years War, he was noted for his chivalry - the code of honour by which he lived. He was known to be hasty at times and rash in some of his engagements yet he was acknowledged as a great man by the people of his own time.

He was probably more like his grandfather, the 'little soldier' whose bravery at the battles of Crecy and Neville's Cross was remarked upon, than his father, the first Earl of Northumberland who, as eldest son of the granddaughter of King Henry III, was more of a courtier and politician. The first Earl Percy was killed in 1408 and his lands and castles were forfeit to the crown but Hotspur's son, Henry, was restored to his inheritance by King Henry V and was created second Earl of Northumberland. He fortified the town of Alnwick with walls and four town gates (or towers) at Bailiffgate, Clayport, Pottergate, and Bondgate,

at the southern entrance to the town, which is known as Hotspur Tower and still straddles the main road as a proud memorial to a renowned border knight.

Bondgate (Hotspur) Tower

Properties Held by the Percies

in England in the Fourteenth Century

Place	County	Acquired
Topcliffe	Yorkshire	1069
Spofford	Yorkshire	1069
Tadcaster	Yorkshire	1120
Petworth	Sussex	1150
Dunsley	York	1200
Sutton upon Derwent	York	1240
Leconfield	York	1240
Mitford	Northumberland	1240
Alnwick	Northumberland	1310
Warkworth	Northumberland	1321
Newburn	Northumberland	1331
Kirk Levington	Yorkshire	1370
Dalton Percy	Durham	1370
Whalram Percy	Yorkshire	1370
Dronfield	Derbyshire	1377
Emelins	Wales	1380
Wressil	Yorkshire	1380
Cockermouth	Cumberland	1385
Egremont	Cumberland	1385
Prudhoe	Northumberland	1392
Langley	Northumberland	1392
The Castle	Isle of Man	1399
Beaumaris	Wales	1399
Northumberland House	The Close, Newcastle	*
Percy's Inn	York	*
Earl's Inn	Newcastle	*
Percy House	Bishopgate, London	*
Northumberland House	Aldgate, London	*
A Mansion	Beverley	*
A Mansion	Durham	*

*Date acquired uncertain

[The Percies also owned estates in Scotland from time to time]

The Percies as Border Wardens

Date	East March	West March
13.7.1377	Earl Percy	
	Thomas Percy	
12.12.1377	Earl Percy	Earl Percy
10.3.1380	Earl Percy	
29.5.1380	Earl Percy	
16.12.1381	Earl Percy(Middle March)	
14.3.1382	Earl Percy	Earl Percy
16.6.1382	Earl Percy(Middle March)	
7.5.1383	Earl Percy	Earl Percy
3.7.1383	Thomas Percy	
	Earl Percy(Middle March)	
12.12.1383	Earl Percy	Earl Percy
12.1.1384	Earl Percy	
	Thomas Percy	
30.7.1384	Earl Percy	Earl Percy
	Henry Percy (Hotspur)	Henry Percy (Hotspur)
1.8.1384	Earl Percy	Earl Percy
20.5.1385	Henry Percy (Hotspur)	
19.6.1388		Henry Percy (Hotspur)
15.6.1390		Henry Percy (Hotspur)
1.6.1391	Earl Percy	
2.6.1396	Henry Percy (Hotspur)	
2.8.1399	Earl Percy	

Genealogy

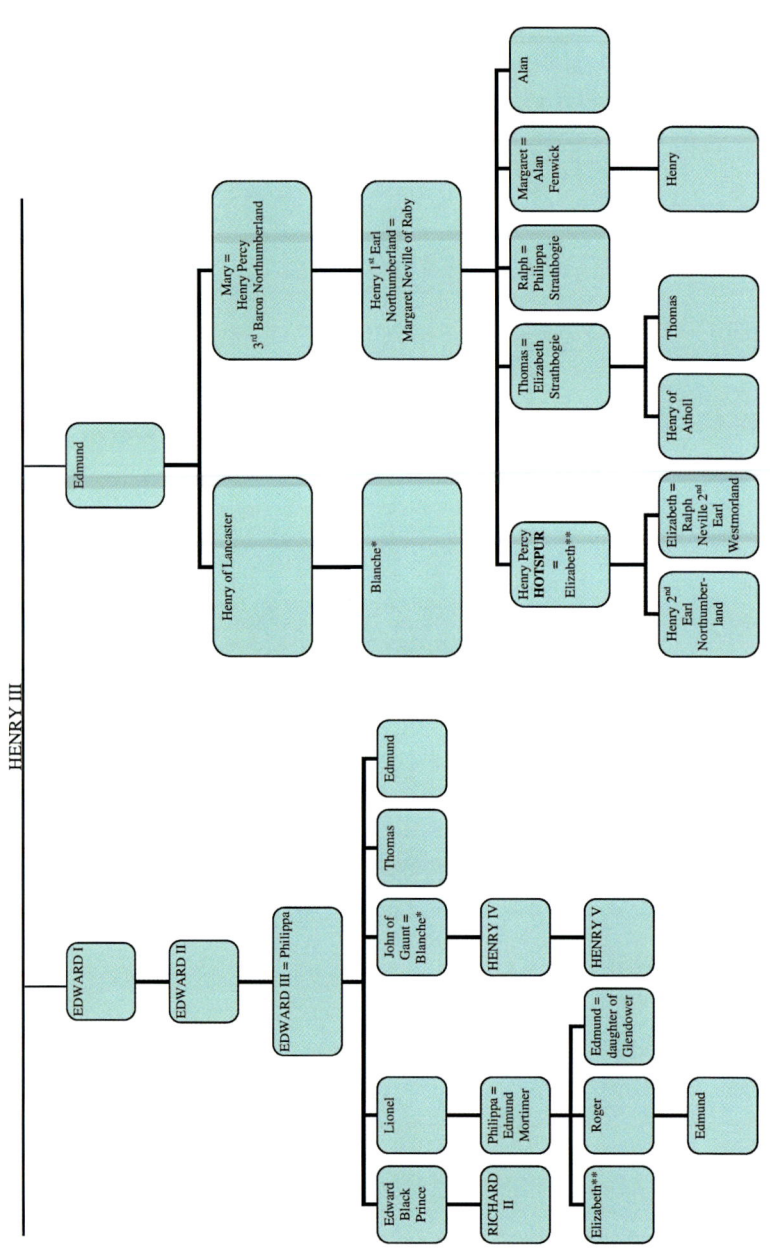

Bibliography

ARCHAELOGIA AELIANA: Series 3, Vol 14

BEAN: Henry IV and the Percies

BRENAN: History of the House of Percy, Vol 1

BURNE: The Battle of Shrewsbury – a military reconstruction

DAVISON: History of Alnwick

DE FONBLANQUE: Annals of the House of Percy, Vol 1

DICTIONARY OF NATIONAL BIOGRAPHY

HARDYNG's Chronicle

HODGSON: History of Northumberland, Vol 5

JACOB: The Fifteenth Century

KIRBY: Henry IV – The Usurper King

MAXWELL: History of the House of Douglas, Vol 1

RIDPATH: Border History

SEWARD: Henry V as Warlord

STOREY: Wardens of the Marches of England towards Scotland

TATE: History of Alnwick, Vol 1

Places to visit

NORTHUMBERLAND

Warkworth
- Castle & Hermitage, English Heritage

Alnwick
- Alnwick Castle, home of the Duke of Northumberland
  - 'Hotspur's seat'
  - Hotspur's Shield
- St Leonard's hospice (ruin)
- Hulne Abbey (ruin)
- Alnwick Abbey Gatehouse
- The Chantry, Walkergate (ruin)

Berwick
- Berwick Castle

Otterburn
- Battle site
- Otterburn Tower

Humbleton (Homildon), nr Wooler
- Battle stone in field next to A697
- Hill walk

NEWCASTLE

West Gate (site of) & small piece of town wall (Westgate Road)
Hotspur pub, Percy Street (nr Haymarket)

SHREWSBURY

Battlefield Church

SCOTLAND

Hailes Castle

WALES

Conwy Castle